P9-BXW-038

THE ULTIMATE CAT TREAT COOKBOOK

by
LIZ PALIKA

Illustrated by
ROY CUMMINGS

HOMEMADE GOODIES
FOR FINICKY FELINES

Howell
Book House™

Howell Book House
Published by Wiley Publishing, Inc., Hoboken, New Jersey

For general information on our other products and services or to obtain technical support please contact our Customer Care Department within the U.S. at (800) 762-2974, outside the U.S. at (317) 572-3993 or fax (317) 572-4002.

Wiley also publishes its books in a variety of electronic formats. Some content that appears in print may not be available in electronic books. For more information about Wiley products, please visit our web site at www.wiley.com.

Library of Congress Cataloging-in-Publication Data available from the publisher upon request.
ISBN-10: 0-471-79255-1
ISBN-13: 978-0-471-79255-0

Printed in the United States of America

10 9 8 7 6 5 4 3 2 1

Book design by LeAndra Hosier
Cover design by Troy Cummings
Cover art by Troy Cummings
Book production by Wiley Publishing, Inc. Composition Services

Table of Contents

Acknowledgments

Thank you to Deb Eldredge, DVM, for scrutinizing all these recipes to make sure our feline friends can safely indulge! Thanks, Deb! I appreciate it.

Thanks, too, to Troy Cummings for his wonderful illustrations. They were a big hit in *The Ultimate Dog Treat Cookbook* and will be just as popular in this book, I'm sure.

Introduction

You have probably heard that cats can be finicky eaters. And many cats are. However, while I was testing recipes for *The Ultimate Dog Treat Cookbook*, my cats were very interested in most of the recipes I was making. Xena, a 4-year-old classic tabby, was insistent that I share some of the treats with her; when I handed a treat to the dogs, she was right there with them, her paw outstretched to bat a treat from my hand. So I began making cat treats, too.

Taste Tests

As I created and tested recipes for this book, I did find that cats can be much pickier than dogs, and each cat had specific likes and dislikes. Xena liked treats that smelled good. If the treat had a strong meaty scent, she would try it. Havoc, my 11-year-old Russian Blue, loves catnip, and any of the treats with catnip garnered his interest. He didn't like soft treats, though; he prefers hard, crunchy ones. Squirt, my 15-year-old, was open-minded; she would sniff anything, but she reliably ate only those treats made with tuna.

Midway through testing the recipes for this book, my husband and I took in two abandoned sister kittens and named them Pumpkin and Squash. (Yes, we adopted them in the fall, and yes, they are orange and white!) Here were two new taste testers for me. Of course, this was a little unfair because the sisters had been hungry, and they were willing to eat just about anything. But if a recipe didn't cut it with these two, I dropped it.

After testing the treats with my cats, I asked some friends with cats to do some taste tests of their own. I would like to thank these people for letting their cats comprise my second round of taste testers: Petra Burke and her two domestic shorthairs, Aspen and Cedar; Katy Silva and her several cats, including Nacho; and Kate Abbott and her two cats, Thomas and Montague. Several other cats also participated in our taste tests, and my thanks go out to all of them. After cats approved these recipes, Deb Eldredge, DVM, scrutinized them to make sure they are indeed safe for our feline friends.

I didn't expect all the cats to like all the treats in this book; that would be expecting too much because cats do have such specific likes and dislikes. However, if several cats disliked a particular treat, I either took that recipe back to the kitchen and revamped it or I dropped the recipe altogether. All the recipes in the book were accepted by the majority of the cats who took part in the testing.

Cooking and Baking Terms

This book is written in an easy-to-understand style, using the following cooking and baking terms:

- **Chop:** To cut food into pieces, from small (finely chopped) to large (coarsely chopped)
- **Dice:** To cut food into equal-sized small cubes (usually between ¼ and ½ inch)
- **Grate:** To shred a solid food by using a hand grater, a blender, or a food processor
- **Knead:** To work dough with your hands, usually on a floured surface, to thoroughly blend the ingredients
- **Puree:** To mash food in a food processor or blender until it becomes a smooth paste or liquid
- **Score:** To cut, with a sharp knife, partway through uncooked dough so that it will break more evenly and easily after baking

Minimum Equipment

You do not need a kitchen full of special gadgets to create great-tasting cat treats, but you do need some basic equipment:

- A large metal or glass bowl for mixing ingredients
- A set of measuring cups that includes ¼ cup, ⅓ cup, ½ cup, and 1 cup
- A set of measuring spoons that includes ¼ teaspoon, 1 teaspoon, and 1 tablespoon
- Two cookie sheets
- A breadboard
- A rolling pin
- Small cookie cutters about 1 inch across (plastic or metal) in any shape

Some of the recipes also call for a food processor or blender. An electric mixer is not required, as most recipes are best mixed by hand.

Some Cooking Tips

If your cat likes crunchy treats, you can make many of the baked treats crunchier by turning off the oven, placing the treats back on a cookie sheet, and returning the treats to the oven for several hours or overnight as the oven cools.

If your cat has an allergy to wheat, including wheat flour, make the recipe with oat flour, rice flour, or even potato flour instead; most of the treats don't require wheat flour. Just watch your baking times as the different flours can bake at slightly different rates. Also, some of the flours can create treats with different textures, so you may need to increase or decrease the moisture in each recipe. Some cats are lactose intolerant, so for those cats, you need to pay attention to which recipes include nonfat dry milk. Most of the recipes that require milk use goat's milk, which is tolerable to more cats than is cow's milk. Chapter 5 includes several additional wheat-free and lactose-free recipes.

Store any treats containing meats or fish in the refrigerator. Left out, they will spoil quickly. To store treats for more than 2 weeks, freeze them in a zipper-top plastic freezer bag or an airtight container.

A Variety of Treats

This cookbook includes recipes for several different forms of treats. Some are dropped by the spoonful onto a cookie sheet, while others are rolled out, cut with cookie cutters, and baked. Some are made from precooked ingredients, and those ingredients are mixed together to create a treat. A few even have raw ingredients. There are also recipes for something called "glop," which is designed to appeal to all cats, even the pickiest eaters.

As you make treats for your cats, keep in mind that treats are not the sole component of a healthy daily diet. Although most of the recipes in this book are made from good foods, they are not designed to replace a quality diet. As a general rule, treats should not exceed 10% of a cat's daily diet.

1

Cookies by the Spoonful

Most of the cookies in this chapter are measured out by the spoonful to make bite-sized treats. You can vary the size of the spoonful, making smaller treats for kittens, small cats, and cats on a diet, or larger treats for bigger cats. If you vary the size from that stated in the recipe, however, watch your baking times. Smaller treats need less baking time, and larger treats need more.

Most of these recipes create a dough that is easily mixed by hand, although you can use a mixer if you wish. Several recipes do call for the use of a food processor or blender.

For recipes calling for baking treats on greased cookie sheets, you can use oil, butter, or nonstick spray. When spooning the dough onto cookie sheets, make uniformly sized treats in each batch. If you make treats of various sizes and bake them on the same cookie sheet, they will bake unevenly; smaller ones may burn and larger ones may not cook completely. While baking any treats, watch them carefully as they bake. Ovens vary, and so do baking times.

Tempting Tuna Treats

∽ Makes 55 to 65 marble-sized treats ∽

To most cats, tuna is almost as attractive as catnip! Tony is an all-black domestic short-hair cat who chose these treats every time during taste tests.

> 1 3-ounce can albacore tuna in water or oil, undrained
> ½ cup whole wheat flour
> ½ cup nonfat dry milk
> 1 tablespoon vegetable oil
> 1 large egg
> ¼ cup water

1. Preheat the oven to 350 degrees.

2. In a large bowl, use a fork to shred the tuna into small pieces.

3. Add the remaining ingredients, mixing well. The dough will be sticky.

4. Flour or oil your hands so you can handle the dough and form the dough into small, marble-sized balls.

5. Place the balls on a greased cookie sheet, and use your fingers to gently flatten them.

6. Bake for about 10 minutes or until the bottoms of the treats are golden brown.

7. Flip the treats and bake for another 5 to 10 minutes or until both sides of the treats are golden brown.

8. Remove from the oven, let cool thoroughly, and store in an airtight container in the refrigerator.

Nutritional Notes: Tuna

Cats love tuna, sometimes to the point of addiction. But even human-grade canned (or fresh) tuna should not be used as a sole food for a cat, no matter how much the cat enjoys it, because eating only tuna can cause a vitamin E deficiency. Tuna also contains insufficient taurine for good health. However, because it is so attractive to cats, it does make an excellent cat treat, and many recipes in this book contain tuna. Most cats enjoy drinking the water drained from a can of tuna packed in water. Just remember that these are treats and not intended to be a complete daily diet.

A 3-ounce can of albacore tuna in water contains:

- 80 calories
- 18 grams protein
- 1 gram fat
- 0 carbohydrates
- 350 mg sodium

Quick and Easy Treats

Makes 12 tablespoon-sized treats

These uncooked treats are quick and easy to make, especially if you have some leftover rice. Serving sizes can vary, from a teaspoon for a kitten or small cat to a tablespoon for a large cat.

> 1 cup cooked green beans
> 1 3-ounce can of your cat's favorite canned cat food
> ⅔ cup cooked rice

1. Place the green beans in a food processor or blender and puree until they form a paste.

2. In a mixing bowl, combine the green bean puree and the other ingredients, mixing well.

3. Refrigerate the mixture in a covered container.

4. To serve, spoon the desired portion (a teaspoonful for a kitten or a tablespoonful for an adult cat) into your cat's bowl.

TREATS AND TIDBITS: STORING TREATS

You can produce the best cat treats in the world, but if you do not store them properly, your efforts will be in vain. Even worse, your cat might get sick if the treats have spoiled.

Before storing treats, make sure they have cooled completely. If they are still warm, moisture will build up in the container, and the treats will soften and perhaps even spoil.

Always store treats in an airtight container, either a plastic bowl with a tight-fitting lid or a zipper-top plastic bag with the air pressed out. Airtight containers seal in freshness and keep moisture out.

Treats containing meats should always be refrigerated after cooling. Simply remove as many treats as you wish to give your cat and then return the rest to the refrigerator. Most meat-based treats in the refrigerator have a shelf life of about 2 weeks. If you want to keep them longer, just pop them in the freezer. Treats can be frozen for up to 4 months.

Simply Special Sardines

 Makes 20 heaping tablespoon-sized treats

This recipe will please every feline fish lover! Serving sizes of this uncooked treat can vary, from a teaspoon for a kitten or small cat to a tablespoon for a large cat.

1 3.75-ounce can sardines in oil, undrained
⅔ cup cooked rice
¼ cup cat grass, finely chopped

1. Place the sardines and their oil in a food processor or blender and puree until smooth.

2. In a mixing bowl, combine the sardine puree and the remaining ingredients, mixing well.

3. Refrigerate in a covered container for up to 1 week. Freeze the excess.

4. To serve, spoon the desired portion (a teaspoonful for a kitten or a tablespoonful for an adult cat) into your cat's bowl.

TREATS AND TIDBITS: CAT GRASS

The term *cat grass* refers to grasses grown indoors, specifically for cats. These grasses can be found as seeds packaged for this purpose or as grasses already sprouted in potting soil and ready for the cat to munch on.

Cat grasses can provide essential fiber for your cat's diet. They can also be something for your cat to play with—part of your environmental enrichment program. If your cat likes to munch on greens, providing her some cat grass may keep her away from your potted plants or from wanting to spend time outside.

The most common seeds used in commercial cat grass preparations include oats, wheat, Japanese millet, and bluegrass. You can also use fescue and ryegrass. Do *not* use sorghum or sudangrass, because they are both poisonous to cats.

Chicken Liver Pate

All our taste-testing cats devoured this recipe with gusto! Serving sizes can vary, from a teaspoon for a kitten or small cat to a tablespoon for a large cat.

> 4 chicken hearts and/or gizzards
> 6 ounces chicken livers
> 1 ounce chicken fat
> 1 large egg
> ½ teaspoon garlic powder

1. Preheat the oven to 350 degrees.

2. Rinse the chicken livers and hearts and/or gizzards. Set aside.

3. Place the chicken fat in a skillet and warm. Add the chicken livers and hearts and/or gizzards. Cook until brown.

4. Place the cooked chicken parts in a food processor. Add the egg and garlic powder. Puree until relatively smooth.

5. Grease two mini loaf pans. Divide the pureed chicken between the two pans.

6. Place a baking pan that is large enough to hold both mini pans in the oven. Fill with about 2 inches of boiling water, and set the two loaf pans in the water.

7. Bake for 30 minutes.

8. Remove from the oven, let cool thoroughly, and store in an airtight container in the refrigerator for up to 1 week. Freeze any excess treats and thaw before serving.

9. To serve, spoon the desired portion (a teaspoonful for a kitten or a tablespoonful for an adult cat) into your cat's bowl.

TREATS AND TIDBITS: CATS ARE CARNIVORES

From the shape of their teeth to the functioning of their bodies and their hunting behaviors, all cats are designed to eat meat. Wild cats catch and eat live prey; you will never see a wild cat harvesting and drying alfalfa for an afternoon snack or boiling a pot of wheat for breakfast. However, it's very difficult to feed our companion cats a balanced diet consisting entirely of meat. Carbohydrates (plant-based foods) make cooking and baking dry cat foods and dry treats much easier. In addition, carbohydrates are inexpensive, especially compared to meat.

When feeding your cat—both her daily foods and her treats—it's important to keep an eye on her diet. Too many carbohydrates can have a detrimental effect on your cat's health. If you have any questions, talk to your veterinarian.

Leftover Magic

Animal behaviorists agree that it's not a good idea to feed your pet (whether cat, dog, bird, or ferret) from the dining room table because it could lead to bad behaviors you'll regret later (begging too much, jumping up on the table, or even stealing food). However, if you have some leftovers, you can share them with your cat by giving them to her in her bowl or from a spoon after you've eaten your meal. Serving sizes for this treat vary from a tablespoon for a kitten to ¼ cup for an adult cat.

½ cup cooked chicken, turkey, fish, or beef

¼ cup cooked rice, sweet potato, squash, or pumpkin (plain, without sugar or seasonings)

¼ cup greens (cat grass, pureed green beans, or finely chopped red or romaine lettuce)

1. Place the meat in a bowl and use a fork to shred it into small pieces.

2. Combine the remaining ingredients and mix gently but thoroughly.

3. Store in a covered container in the refrigerator for up to 1 week.

4. To serve, spoon the desired portion (a tablespoonful for a kitten or ¼ cup for an adult cat) into your cat's bowl.

Ooh la la, Oysters!

Makes about 40 ½-teaspoon-sized treats

Oysters for your cat? Why not? These treats were eagerly eaten by most of our test cats and throughout our taste tests were one of the favorites.

1 3.75-ounce can oysters
6 baby carrots
2 tablespoons tomato paste
1 large egg
⅓ cup plain, unseasoned bread crumbs
2 teaspoons brewer's yeast

1. Preheat the oven to 350 degrees.

2. Place the oysters, carrots, and tomato paste in a food processor or blender and puree until they form a smooth paste.

3. In a mixing bowl, combine the pureed mixture and the remaining ingredients, mixing well.

4. Drop by ½ teaspoonful onto a greased cookie sheet.

5. Bake for 8 to 12 minutes or until the bottoms of the treats are golden brown.

6. Flip the treats and bake for another 5 minutes or until both sides are golden brown.

7. Remove from the oven, let cool thoroughly, and store in an airtight container in the refrigerator.

Wake Up, Sleepyhead!

This is a wonderful treat to start the day! You can use leftover eggs from your breakfast or scramble a fresh one. All our taste-tester cats enjoyed this easy-to-make treat. Because of its appeal, you can also use these delectables as training treats.

⅓ cup scrambled eggs
¼ cup finely grated cheddar cheese
1 3-ounce can of your cat's favorite canned cat food

1. Place all the ingredients in a food processor or blender and puree until they form a coarse paste.

2. Store in an airtight container in the refrigerator for up to 3 days.

3. Serve by the tablespoonful in your cat's bowl.

NUTRITIONAL NOTES: PROTEIN

Complete proteins, which contain all the amino acids needed for good feline health, can be found in meats, eggs, fish, milk, and other dairy products. Incomplete proteins, those that are lacking one or more of the essential amino acids, are found in beans, peanuts (and other nuts), grains, and potatoes (including sweet potatoes). As true carnivores, cats require more essential amino acids than dogs, so meats and other sources of complete proteins are even more important to a cat's diet than to a dog's.

Proteins are needed for all the functions of life, including growth, repair of injuries, energy, and much more. One gram of protein supplies the body with 4 calories, the same as 1 gram of carbohydrates.

Bisquick and Beef

Bake these treats just until the bottoms begin to turn golden brown. When these treats were overbaked, our taste-tester cats turned up their noses; when baked for a shorter period of time and still somewhat soft, the treats were eagerly eaten.

⅔ cup cooked beef
1 large egg
⅓ cup Bisquick baking mix
1 tablespoon water

1. Preheat the oven to 350 degrees.

2. Place the beef and egg in a food processor or blender and puree until they form a thick paste.

3. In a mixing bowl, combine the meat and egg mixture with the Bisquick and water, mixing well.

4. Drop by ½ teaspoonful onto a greased cookie sheet.

5. Bake for 5 to 7 minutes or until bottoms of the treats just begin to turn golden brown.

6. Remove from the oven, let cool thoroughly, and store in an airtight container in the refrigerator.

Nutritional Notes: Bisquick

Bisquick is a staple in many households. It can be used for making coffee cakes, pancakes, and many other human treats. Although there are no cat treat recipes listed on the box, Bisquick can be a great base for cat treat recipes. Bisquick contains all-purpose flour, with added vitamins, oil, baking soda, sugar, and salt. Bisquick is a convenience food for cat treat bakers because it already contains many of the ingredients you might use in a recipe. If your cat is on a low-sodium diet, however, do not use Bisquick.

⅓ cup of Bisquick contains:

- 160 calories
- 3 grams protein
- 6 grams fat
- 26 grams carbohydrates
- 1 gram sugar
- 35 mg potassium
- 490 mg sodium

Bountiful Banana Treats

This treat is made using Prowl, a dehydrated cat food made by The Honest Kitchen (see next page).

⅓ cup Prowl
⅓ cup warm water
1 tablespoon sour cream
½ average-sized banana, mashed
⅓ cup rice flour

1. Preheat the oven to 350 degrees.

2. Put the Prowl in a small bowl. Add the warm water, stir, and allow the Prowl to rehydrate for 5 minutes.

3. In a mixing bowl, combine the rehydrated Prowl, the sour cream, and the banana, mixing well.

4. Stir in the rice flour.

5. Drop by ½ teaspoonful onto a greased cookie sheet.

6. Bake for 8 to 10 minutes or until the bottoms of the treats are golden brown.

7. Remove from the oven, let cool thoroughly, and store in an airtight container in the refrigerator.

Apple Treats: Although most cats like banana, if you find your cat turning up her nose at it, you can substitute ⅓ cup unsweetened applesauce for the banana in this recipe.

NUTRITIONAL NOTES: PROWL

Prowl is a dehydrated cat food made by The Honest Kitchen in San Diego, California (www.the honestkitchen.com). Prowl contains 100% human-grade chicken, eggs, potatoes, yams, organic flaxseed, zucchini, spinach, honey, cranberries, and rosemary.

The guaranteed analysis of Prowl is:

- Protein: minimum 32%
- Fat: minimum 28%
- Fiber: maximum 2.5%
- Moisture: maximum 4.2%
- Calcium: minimum 0.9%, maximum 1.0%
- Phosphorus: minimum 0.78%, maximum 0.80%
- Sodium: minimum 0.2%, maximum 0.38%
- Magnesium: minimum 0.07%, maximum 0.09%
- Taurine: minimum 0.12%, maximum 0.14%
- Calories: 5,070 per kg
- Carbohydrates: 29%

Chicken and Stars

This easy-to-make recipe is tasty and appealing to most cats. When you measure out the condensed chicken soup, do not dilute it with water; use it in the recipe in its condensed form.

> ½ cup Campbell's Chicken and Stars condensed soup
> 1 cup all-purpose flour
> 1 large egg

1. Preheat the oven to 350 degrees.

2. In a mixing bowl, combine all the ingredients until well mixed.

3. Drop by teaspoonful onto a greased cookie sheet.

4. Bake for 8 to 10 minutes or until the bottoms of the treats are just turning golden brown.

5. Remove from the oven, let cool thoroughly, and store in an airtight container in the refrigerator.

6. To serve, break each treat into bite-sized pieces.

Tempting Chicken Soup Snacks

Makes 80 to 100 bite-sized treats

These are soft cookies with a strong chicken flavor that will tempt even the most finicky cat! Amber, a 3-year-old orange shorthaired female, gobbled these up. The serving size can be one snack for a full-grown cat or half a snack for a smaller cat or kitten.

> 1 cup high-quality chicken-based dry cat food
> 2 cups Bisquick baking mix
> 1 18.8-ounce can Campbell's Chunky Chicken soup

1. Preheat the oven to 350 degrees.

2. Place the cat food in a food processor or blender and grind to a coarse powder. Measure 1 cup after grinding.

3. In a large bowl, combine the ground cat food and the remaining ingredients, mixing well.

4. Drop by teaspoonful onto a greased cookie sheet.

5. Score each cookie in half.

6. Bake for 8 to 12 minutes or until the bottoms of the treats begin to turn golden brown.

7. Remove from the oven, let cool thoroughly, and store in an airtight container in the refrigerator.

Italian Goodies

Makes 40 to 50 bite-sized treats

These goodies have a great tomato and Parmesan cheese odor and taste.

½ cup high-quality dry cat food
2 cups finely shredded, cooked ground beef
¼ cup grated carrot
½ cup canned grated Parmesan cheese
1 large egg
1 tablespoon tomato paste

1. Preheat the oven to 350 degrees.

2. Put the cat food in a food processor or blender and grind to a coarse powder. Measure ½ cup after grinding.

3. In a mixing bowl, combine all the ingredients, mixing thoroughly.

4. Form the dough into marble-sized balls.

5. Bake for 10 to 12 minutes or until the bottoms of the treats are golden brown.

6. Remove from the oven, let cool thoroughly, and store in an airtight container in the refrigerator.

Treats and Tidbits: Helping the Overweight Cat

Obesity is the number-one problem most veterinarians see in cats today. Obesity can lead to a variety of health problems, including joint pain and disorders, as well as diabetes. You can help your cat slim down by taking a few steps:

- Feed a good-quality food.
- Feed at certain times of the day instead of leaving the food out all day to keep your cat from free feeding all day.
- Measure how much food you give your cat. She needs to feel full yet not overindulge.
- Make sure all treats are low fat and limit how many treats your cat eats each day.
- Increase your cat's activities. Find some good toys to increase her desire to play. Wake her up and have her walk around the house. Put up a birdfeeder outside a window so she has something interesting to watch.

Yummy Chicken Liver Balls

❧ Makes 50 to 55 pea- to marble-sized treats ☙

Squash, a 4-month-old orange-and-white kitten, prowled the kitchen, crying, when these treats were being made.

> 1 pound finely chopped cooked chicken livers
> 1 cup cornmeal
> ¾ cup all-purpose flour
> 2 large eggs
> ¼ cup chicken broth

1. Preheat the oven to 350 degrees.

2. Combine all the ingredients, making sure the chicken liver is well coated. The dough should be stiff, but if it's too dry, add a little more chicken broth.

3. Form the dough into pea- to marble-sized balls and place on a greased cookie sheet.

4. With the tip of a spoon, press a tiny indentation into the top of each ball.

5. With a spoon, carefully drip a few drops of chicken broth in each indentation.

6. Bake the treats for 8 to 10 minutes or until the bottoms of the treats are golden brown.

7. Remove from the oven, let cool thoroughly, and store in an airtight container in the refrigerator.

Nutritional Notes: Corn and Cornmeal

Corn originated in Central America and was a food staple for thousands of years, although not in the form we see today. Today's corn is a much larger plant, and the ears are huge compared to the ears of yesteryear. Today, corn is a high-fiber, high-carbohydrate food that is also a source of vitamin C and some of the B vitamins. Cornmeal is made from dried corn kernels. Although many cats eat corn and cornmeal with no problem (it's in many dry cat foods), some cats cannot tolerate it and develop a food allergy. If your cat is allergic to corn, avoid the recipes containing corn or cornmeal.

1 cup of cornmeal contains:

- 490 calories
- 12 grams protein
- 2 grams fat
- 100 grams carbohydrates
- 450 mg calcium
- 858 mg phosphorus
- 57 RE vitamin A
- 1 mg thiamin
- 1 mg riboflavin

2

Cookie-Cutter Treats

A dog treat shaped like a bone is recognizable as a treat, and most dogs eagerly gobble them down. Cats, however, need much smaller treats than dogs, and there is no universal shape for cats' cookies. Because cats have teeth designed to catch, hold, and eat prey (meat), cat treats should be made in a size or shape that the cat can crunch in one bite or grip and bite into smaller pieces. When you choose cookie cutters, find the smallest ones available, preferably 1 inch across or even smaller. The shape is unimportant; your cat won't care if the treat is shaped like a flower or a fish.

After rolling out the dough and cutting out the first batch of treats, gather the leftover dough scraps, form another ball, and roll out as before. Cut out the remaining cookies, placing them on the cookie sheet.

Most of these recipes recommend scoring each treat so that it can be easily broken into smaller treats. To score a cookie-cutter treat, after the treat has been cut out of the rolled dough, use a knife to draw a line or two across each treat, cutting about halfway through the dough. Once baked, the treats will easily break along the scored lines.

The baking times given are for the thickness of dough mentioned in each recipe and for treats cut out with 1-inch-wide cookie cutters. If you roll the dough to a different thickness or use a cookie cutter of a different size, you need to change the baking times. Watch the treats as they are baking and take them out when they are golden brown.

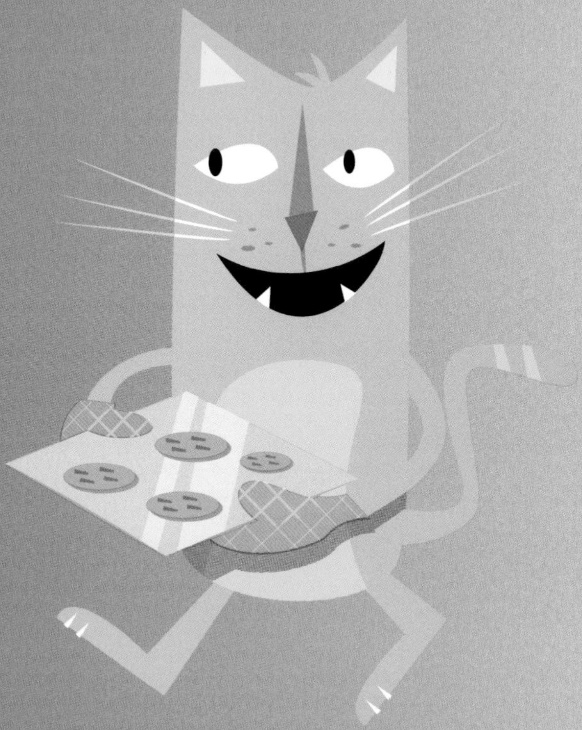

Basic Kitty Cookies

Makes 35 1-inch cookies

This is a basic recipe for good-tasting cookies. When it is made as is, cats enjoy the beefy taste. However, this recipe can easily be varied to create different tastes, depending on your cat's likes and dislikes.

> ½ cup high-quality dry cat food
> 1 cup all-purpose flour
> ½ teaspoon salt
> ½ teaspoon baking soda
> 1 large egg
> ¼ cup beef broth
> ¼ cup flour, for rolling out treats

1. Preheat the oven to 350 degrees.

2. In a mixing bowl, combine the first four ingredients, mixing well.

3. Add the egg and beef broth, mixing well.

4. Sprinkle the remaining ¼ cup flour on a breadboard. Roll out the dough in the flour until it is ¼ inch thick.

5. Use a 1-inch cookie cutter to cut out the cookies.

6. Place the cut-out cookies on a greased cookie sheet.

7. Score all cookies with a sharp knife, creating a + on each cookie.

8. With a spoon, carefully drip a few drops of beef broth on the top of each cookie.

9. Bake for 8 to 10 minutes or until the bottoms of the treats are just turning golden brown.

10. Remove from the oven, let cool thoroughly, and store in an airtight container.

11. Serve as a 1-inch cookie or break each cookie into four pieces along the scored lines.

Crunchier Treats: If your cat loves crunchier treats, when all the cookies have been baked, turn off the oven. Place all the cookies back on a cookie sheet and return them to the oven. Leave the cookies in the cooling oven for several hours or overnight.

Chicken Cookies: If your cat likes chicken, substitute chicken broth for the beef broth.

Bacon Cookies: If your cat loves bacon, use water in the recipe instead of beef broth. Prior to baking, drip a few drops of bacon grease on the top of each cookie.

Tuna Cookies: For tasty tuna cookies, use the water drained from a can of tuna packed in water in place of the beef broth.

Salmon Cookies: For a salmon-loving kitty, use the juice from a can of salmon in place of the beef broth.

Low-Salt Bouillon Cookies: For cats who must adhere to a low-sodium diet, use low-salt bouillon (beef or chicken) in place of the beef broth.

Chicken Liver Crunchies

Charlene, a 14-year-old silver Persian, is quite particular about her food and treats but eagerly eats these every time they are offered.

½ cup cooked chicken livers
½ cup warm water
¼ cup finely grated carrots
1¼ cups whole wheat flour
1 tablespoon vegetable oil
¼ cup flour, for rolling out treats
¼ cup dried catnip, for rolling out treats

1. Preheat the oven to 350 degrees.

2. Place the cooked chicken livers, water, and carrots in a food processor or blender and blend to a thick paste.

3. In a mixing bowl, combine the chicken liver paste with the 1¼ cups whole wheat flour and the oil, mixing well. The dough will be sticky.

4. Sprinkle the catnip and the ¼ cup flour on a breadboard, combining them lightly with your fingers.

5. Roll out the dough in the flour and catnip until the dough is ¼ inch thick.

6. Use a 1-inch cookie cutter to cut out the treats; place the cut-out treats close together on a greased cookie sheet. (These treats will not rise or spread.)

7. If your cat likes smaller treats, score all the cookies with a sharp knife, creating a + on each cookie so that it can be broken after baking.

8. Bake for 5 to 7 minutes or until the bottoms of the treats are golden brown.

9. Flip the treats and bake for another 5 minutes or until both sides of the treats are golden brown.

10. Remove from the oven, let cool thoroughly, and store in an airtight container in the refrigerator. Freeze excess treats for up to several months.

Crunchier Treats: If your cat loves crunchier treats, when all the cookies have been baked, turn off the oven. Place all the cookies back on a cookie sheet and return them to the oven. Leave the cookies in the cooling oven for several hours or overnight.

Tuna Stars

Makes 85 to 95 1-inch stars

These cookies are cut out using a 1-inch star cookie cutter. The star's small body and long arms give the cat a good grip for crunching. Therefore, these treats do not need to be scored or broken into pieces.

1 6-ounce can albacore tuna in water, undrained
1¼ cups all-purpose flour
2 large eggs
¼ cup flour, for rolling out treats

1. Preheat the oven to 350 degrees.

2. Put the tuna and water from the can into a bowl. Use a fork to shred the tuna into fine pieces.

3. Add the 1¼ cup flour and eggs, mixing well.

4. Sprinkle the ¼ cup flour on a breadboard. Roll out the dough in the flour until the dough is about ¼ inch thick.

5. Use a 1-inch star-shaped cookie cutter to cut out the treats; place the cut-out treats on a greased cookie sheet.

6. Bake for about 8 to 10 minutes, watching to make sure the arms of the stars do not burn.

7. Remove from the oven, let cool thoroughly, and store in an airtight container in the refrigerator.

TREATS AND TIDBITS: ALL ABOUT FLOUR

Flour is made by grinding or pulverizing grains and other plants, but all flours are not the same. The most popular flours are wheat flours; most flours sold in grocery stores for baking are bleached (chemically treated with benzoyl peroxide or similar chemicals) wheat flours. The more natural unbleached wheat flours are gaining in popularity, though. Flours can be made from many plants—from wheat to rye and from potatoes to garbanzo beans. If your cat has a food allergy to wheat, you can use one of the many alternatives.

Here are the most common flours:

- **All-purpose flour:** Contains both protein-rich hard wheat and starch-rich soft wheat.
- **Durum flour:** A high-gluten flour made from hard durum wheat. (Gluten is the combination of two proteins: gliadin and glutenin.)
- **Garbanzo flour:** A flour made from dried garbanzo beans, also known as chickpeas.
- **Gluten flour:** Dehydrated gluten is added to make this high-protein flour, often 40% protein.
- **Gluten-free flour:** Contains no gluten and is often made from potato starch, garbanzo, and other flours.
- **Potato starch flour:** A gluten-free flour made from potatoes.
- **Rye flour:** Made from rye, a grass.
- **Soy flour:** A high-protein flour made from roasted soybeans.
- **Whole wheat flour:** Contains the germ, bran, and husk of the wheat seed.

Puff Pastry Hearts

Makes 18 to 21 1-inch treats

These are easy to make yet very special treats. All of our taste-tester cats ate these treats with gusto! Frozen puff pastry can be found in the frozen desserts section at your grocery store.

1 6-ounce can albacore tuna in water, drained
¼ cup flour, for rolling out treats
1 piece of frozen puff pastry, partially thawed (just enough so that it can be handled without breaking)

1. Preheat the oven to 350 degrees.

2. In a small bowl, use a fork to shred the tuna into fine pieces.

3. Sprinkle the flour on a breadboard.

4. Place the pastry on the breadboard and cut it in half.

5. Spread the tuna evenly over one piece of pastry.

6. Place the piece of pastry without the tuna on top of the one with the tuna.

7. Use a 1-inch heart-shaped cookie cutter to cut out the treats, making sure to press the cookie cutter through all the layers.

8. Place the cut-out treats on a greased cookie sheet. Set aside the leftover dough.

9. Bake for 15 to 20 minutes or until golden brown.

10. Remove from the oven, let cool thoroughly, and store in an airtight container in the refrigerator. Serve each cookie whole or break into smaller pieces.

11. Place the leftover dough on a greased cookie sheet. The dough can be one big tangled mess or in several pieces.

12. Bake for 25 to 30 minutes (because it is a larger piece of dough) or until golden brown.

13. Remove from the oven, let cool thoroughly, and store in an airtight container in the refrigerator. Break into small pieces to serve.

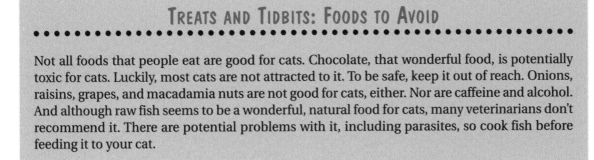

TREATS AND TIDBITS: FOODS TO AVOID

Not all foods that people eat are good for cats. Chocolate, that wonderful food, is potentially toxic for cats. Luckily, most cats are not attracted to it. To be safe, keep it out of reach. Onions, raisins, grapes, and macadamia nuts are not good for cats, either. Nor are caffeine and alcohol. And although raw fish seems to be a wonderful, natural food for cats, many veterinarians don't recommend it. There are potential problems with it, including parasites, so cook fish before feeding it to your cat.

Salmon Soy Circles

Makes 75 to 85 1-inch circular treats

You can find soy flour at your local grocery store—in either the baking section or the health food section. It adds a different texture to baked cookies, and it's a good substitute if your cat is allergic to wheat.

1 7-ounce can salmon in oil, undrained
1½ cups soy flour
2 large eggs
½ cup dried catnip, for rolling out treats
¼ cup flour, for rolling out treats

1. Preheat the oven to 350 degrees.

2. Place the salmon and the oil contained in the can into a mixing bowl. Use a fork to shred the salmon into small pieces.

3. Add the soy flour and eggs, mixing well.

4. Mix the catnip and the ¼ cup flour on a breadboard.

5. Place the dough in the flour and catnip and work it into a ball. Roll it out to about ¼ inch thick.

6. Use a 1-inch circular cookie cutter to cut out the cookies. Place the cut-out cookies on a greased cookie sheet.

7. Score all cookies with a sharp knife, creating a + on each cookie.

8. Bake for 10 to 13 minutes or until the bottoms are just turning golden brown.

9. Remove from the oven, let cool thoroughly, and store in an air-tight container in the refrigerator.

10. Serve each cookie whole or break into smaller pieces along the scored lines.

NUTRITIONAL NOTES: SALMON

Salmon is a favorite food for most cats, second only to tuna. High in protein and fish oils, salmon provides excellent nutrition for active cats; the oils are wonderful for the skin and coat. Concerns have been raised about the safety of farm-raised salmon, so the following statistics apply to healthy, wild-caught salmon.

3 ounces of baked salmon, in natural oils, contains:

- 140 calories
- 18 grams protein
- 6 grams fat
- 0 grams carbohydrates
- 10 mg calcium
- 170 mg phosphorus
- 415 mg potassium
- 37 mg sodium

Tomato Tuna Surprise

⌒🐾 Makes 40 to 45 1-inch treats 🐾⌒

These treats have a different taste and texture than some of the other treats in this chapter, and some of our taste-testing cats were hesitant about them. After the cats tasted the treats, they polished them off with enthusiasm.

1 6-ounce can albacore tuna in water, undrained
2 tablespoons canned kidney beans
1 tablespoon tomato paste
⅓ cup grated mozzarella cheese
1 tablespoon goat's milk
½ cup all-purpose flour
½ cup plain, unseasoned bread crumbs, for rolling out treats
¼ cup flour, for rolling out treats

1. Preheat the oven to 350 degrees.

2. Place the tuna, kidney beans, and tomato paste in a food processor and puree to a coarse paste.

3. In a mixing bowl, combine the tuna paste with the cheese and goat's milk, mixing well.

4. Stir in the ½ cup flour. The dough will be sticky; add more flour if needed to handle the dough.

5. Mix the breadcrumbs and the ¼ cup flour on a breadboard.

6. Roll out the dough on the bread crumbs and flour until the dough is about ¼ inch thick, turning the dough several times so the dough is well covered.

7. Use a 1-inch cookie cutter to cut out the cookies. Place the cut-out cookies on a greased cookie sheet.

8. Score all cookies with a sharp knife, creating a + on each cookie.

9. Bake for 8 to 10 minutes or until the bottoms of the treats are reddish-golden brown.

10. Remove from the oven, let cool thoroughly, and store in an airtight container in the refrigerator.

11. Serve each cookie whole or break into smaller pieces along the scored lines.

Carrot Snacks

These snacks are colorful, crispy, and tasty. They are also a great source of fiber.

½ cup high-quality dry cat food
2 cups grated carrots
½ cup unsweetened applesauce (no cinnamon)
½ cup plain yogurt
2 cups all-purpose flour
1 teaspoon baking powder
¼ cup flour, for rolling out treats

1. Preheat the oven to 350 degrees.

2. Place the cat food in a food processor or blender and grind to a coarse powder. Measure ½ cup after grinding.

3. Place the carrots in the food processor and puree.

4. Add the applesauce and yogurt to the food processor and puree again until the mixture is smooth.

5. Spoon the pureed mixture into a bowl. Add the 2 cups flour, ground cat food, and baking powder. Mix until a dough forms and then knead with your hands until well mixed. If the dough is too sticky, add a little more flour.

6. Sprinkle the ¼ cup flour on a breadboard.

7. Place the dough on the floured breadboard and roll out to slightly thicker than ¼ inch. The dough will be soft; don't roll it too thin.

8. Use a 1-inch cookie cutter to cut out the cookies. Place the cut-out cookies on a greased cookie sheet.

9. Bake for 5 to 7 minutes or until the bottoms are just beginning to turn golden brown.

10. Flip the treats and bake for another 3 to 5 minutes or until golden brown.

11. Remove from the oven, let cool thoroughly, and store in an airtight container.

Crunchier Treats: If your cat loves crunchier treats, when all the cookies have been baked, turn off the oven. Place all the cookies back on a cookie sheet and return them to the oven. Leave the cookies in the cooling oven for several hours or overnight.

NUTRITIONAL NOTES: FELINES AND SUGAR

You may have noticed that none of the recipes in this book contains sugar, even when sugar might seem to fit. That's because studies have shown that not only do cats not metabolize sugar, they also lack a sweet-receptor gene. The lack of this gene could have caused cats to continue their evolution as true carnivores, whereas canines are behaviorally omnivores—eating both meats and carbohydrates. The gene in cats may have become inactive or defective from lack of use. Thus, no sugars are included in these recipes.

Bacon Circles

⌒ Makes 35 1-inch cookies ⌒

Bacon is not considered a health food (for people or cats!), but that doesn't take away its rich and distinctive taste. Cats who love to share your Sunday morning bacon and eggs will enjoy this treat.

½ cup high-quality dry cat food
1 cup all-purpose flour
½ teaspoon salt
½ teaspoon baking soda
1 large egg
½ cup cooked, finely crumbled bacon
¼ cup warm water
¼ cup flour, for rolling out treats
1 tablespoon bacon grease

1. Preheat the oven to 350 degrees.

2. In a small bowl, mix the first four ingredients.

3. Add the egg, crumbled bacon, and warm water, mixing well.

4. Sprinkle the ¼ cup flour on a breadboard.

5. Place the dough on the floured breadboard and turn it over a couple times as you knead it, making sure the ingredients are well mixed and the dough is covered lightly in flour.

6. Roll out the dough to about ¼ inch thick.

7. Use a 1-inch cookie cutter to cut out the cookies. Place the cut-out cookies on a greased cookie sheet.

8. Score all cookies with a sharp knife, creating a + on each cookie.

9. With a spoon, carefully drip a few drops of bacon grease on top of each cookie.

10. Bake for about 10 minutes or until the bottoms of the treats are golden brown.

11. Remove from the oven, let cool thoroughly, and store in an airtight container in the refrigerator.

12. Serve each cookie whole or break into smaller pieces along the scored lines.

Crunchier Treats: If your cat loves crunchier treats, when all the cookies have been baked, turn off the oven. Place all the cookies back on a cookie sheet and return them to the oven. Leave the cookies in the cooling oven for several hours or overnight.

3

Special Goodies
for Special Occasions

● ●

CERTAIN HOLIDAYS BRING TO MIND SOME SPECIFIC SPECIAL FOODS. TURKEY, OF COURSE, IS ASSOCIATED WITH THANKSGIVING, AND PICNICS MAKE US THINK OF THE FOURTH OF JULY. MY FAMILY LOVES TO SERVE ROAST BEEF ON CHRISTMAS. CHRISTMAS IN OUR FAMILY IS ALSO PRECEDED BY LOTS OF BAKING: COOKIES, BREADS, COFFEE CAKES, AND PET TREATS.

FOOD HAS BEEN AN INTEGRAL PART OF HUMAN CELEBRATIONS FOR AS LONG AS WE'VE RECORDED HISTORY. WE SHARE FOOD WITH GUESTS, AND FOOD MARKS SPECIAL EVENTS. MANY CAT OWNERS ENJOY SHARING SPECIAL OCCASIONS WITH THEIR TREASURED FELINE COMPANIONS, BUT THE FOOD PEOPLE EAT IS NOT ALWAYS GOOD FOR CATS TO EAT. GASTROINTESTINAL UPSET CAN FOLLOW A FEAST OF UNFAMILIAR FOODS, AND THAT'S A SURE WAY TO RUIN A CAT'S (AND A CAT LOVER'S) DAY.

HERE ARE SOME RECIPES THAT YOUR CAT CAN SAFELY INDULGE IN WHILE STILL SHARING THE CELEBRATIONS OF THE DAY.

A FEW RECIPES IN THIS CHAPTER CALL FOR PREMADE DOUGH. FOR EXAMPLE, THE RECIPE FOR THE SURPRISE IS INSIDE! USES CANNED PIZZA DOUGH. USING THIS EASILY FOUND AND INEXPENSIVE DOUGH VASTLY REDUCES THE TIME AND EFFORT NEEDED TO CREATE THE TREAT, ESPECIALLY IF YOU ALREADY HAVE THE DOUGH IN YOUR REFRIGERATOR.

Happy Birthday Catnip Tea

Every cat needs to celebrate her birthday! Here's an extra-special birthday treat. Catnip is an herb in the mint family. The leaves are downy and heart-shaped, and they have a minty smell. Most commercial catnip treats and toys contain dried leaves (and sometimes seeds). Some cats are very attracted to the leaves and like to rub and roll on them and even eat them. But not all cats are attracted to catnip. Very young and very old cats seem to be the least affected. Catnip's appeal is not just for housecats; many larger cats—even tigers—like catnip!

> 1 cup warm water
> 3 tablespoons dried or fresh catnip
> ¼ teaspoon powdered chicken bouillon

1. Place the warm water in a container that has a tight-fitting lid.

2. Add the catnip and chicken bouillon.

3. Shake vigorously for a couple minutes or until the bouillon is dissolved and the catnip has given the tea a greenish tinge.

4. Serve ¼ cup of the tea to your cat in a shallow bowl.

5. Store the remainder in the refrigerator. Warm before serving.

Catnip Tea with Broth or Soup: If you have some chicken broth or soup on hand, substitute either for the powdered bouillon and water.

Squirt's Favorite Birthday Treat

◁ⓒ Makes 6 servings ⓓ▷

If your cat likes catnip, these treats are great for her birthday celebration. Squirt, a 15-year-old orange-and-white domestic shorthair, loves these treats—so much so that she will tear the paper cup off all by herself.

⅓ cup plain yogurt
1 heaping tablespoon dried catnip

1. Stir the catnip into the yogurt, mixing well.

2. Using six 3-ounce mini paper cups, divide the mixture between the cups.

3. Place the cups in the freezer until the treats are frozen, usually a couple hours.

4. To serve, pop a treat out of the cup or tear the cup off. The treat can be messy as it thaws, so serve it on a small plate or be prepared to clean the floor afterward.

Happy Birthday Treats

Makes 18 to 21 1-inch cookies

These birthday treats are perfect for a celebration honoring a treasured feline companion.

¼ cup flour, for rolling out treats

1 piece of frozen puff pastry, thawed partially (until it can be easily handled without breaking)

1 3-ounce can high-quality cat food

1. Preheat the oven to 350 degrees.

2. Sprinkle the flour on a breadboard.

3. Place the pastry on the floured breadboard and cut it in half.

4. Spread 1 tablespoon of the cat food on one piece of pastry, spreading it thinly over the entire piece. This will be the top piece.

5. Spread the remainder of the cat food evenly over the other piece, which will be the bottom.

6. Place the top piece, cat food side up, on the bottom piece.

7. Use a 1-inch cookie cutter to carefully cut out the cookies, cutting through all the layers. Set aside the leftover dough.

8. Place the cookies on a greased cookie sheet.

9. Bake for 15 to 20 minutes or until golden brown.

10. Remove from the oven, let cool thoroughly, and store in an airtight container in the refrigerator. Serve each cookie whole or break into smaller pieces.

11. Place the dough that was left over from cutting out the cookies on a greased cookie sheet. The dough can be one big tangled mess or in several pieces.

12. Bake for 25 to 30 minutes (because it is a larger piece of dough) or until golden brown.

13. Remove from the oven, let cool thoroughly, and store in an airtight container in the refrigerator. Break into small pieces to serve.

The Surprise Is Inside!

ꙅ Makes about 200 ½-inch squares ꙅ

These treats are easy to make, and the recipe produces a lot of them. They can be frozen in small batches and will stay good in the freezer for 2 to 3 months.

1 can pizza dough
1 can Fancy Feast Tuna and Oceanfish Feast in Aspic cat food

1. Preheat the oven to 350 degrees.

2. Remove the pizza dough from the can and cut it in half before unrolling.

3. Unroll the two pieces of dough.

4. Spread ½ of the can of cat food over half of one of the pieces of dough.

5. Fold the dough over the cat food, as if you're making a turnover. Use the tines of a fork to seal the edges.

6. Repeat with the second piece of dough and the remainder of the cat food.

7. Place both cat food turnovers on a greased cookie sheet.

8. Bake for 15 minutes or until golden brown.

9. Remove from the oven, let cool thoroughly, and cut into ½-inch square pieces. Store some of the treats in an airtight container in the refrigerator and the remainder in the freezer.

A Different Cat Food Surprise: Does your cat have a special food that brings her running when you open the can? You can use your cat's favorite canned cat food in place of the Fancy Feast.

Baby Food Surprise: Many cats believe baby food was made for four-legged friends, not two-legged human offspring! If your cat is one of them, instead of the Fancy Feast, substitute a jar of baby food in a meat flavor your cat likes.

Scrambled Eggs Surprise: If your cat stares fixedly at your plate as you eat breakfast on Sunday mornings, scramble one egg and bake it in the turnover in place of the Fancy Feast. You can also crumble a piece of cooked bacon and add it to the eggs.

Frozen Tuna Cow

Makes 6 servings

On a hot summer day, these treats will cool off even the hottest cat!

1 tablespoon albacore tuna in oil or water, drained
⅓ cup plain yogurt

1. Put the tuna in a small bowl and use a fork to shred it into small pieces.

2. Add the yogurt, mixing well.

3. Using six 3-ounce mini paper cups, divide the mixture between the cups.

4. Place the cups in the freezer until the treats are frozen, usually a couple hours.

5. To serve, pop a treat out of the cup or tear the cup off. The treat can be messy as it thaws, so serve it on a small plate or be prepared to clean the floor afterward.

Nutritional Notes: Yogurt

Yogurt is made from fermented milk. Although once referred to as a health food eaten only by health fanatics, it has now found its place in mainstream nutrition. An excellent and nutritious food on its own, yogurt containing live active cultures of *lactobacillus bulgaricus* or *streptococcus thermaphilus* is known to be effective at containing "bad" bacteria in the body, especially in the gastrointestinal and reproductive systems. Yogurt is also extremely effective at helping a sick cat recover while using a course of antibiotics because it adds "good" bacteria to the digestive tract.

Here is a short course on yogurt:

- **Nonfat yogurt:** Made from skim milk containing less than 0.5% fat.
- **Lowfat yogurt:** Made from lowfat or part skim milk containing 0.5% to 2% fat.
- **Whole milk yogurt:** Made from whole milk with at least 3.25% milk fat.
- **Contains active yogurt cultures:** Yogurt that is not heat treated after culturing and therefore contains active bacterial cultures.
- **Heat treated after culturing:** Yogurt that has been heat treated after culturing to prolong shelf life. It contains no active bacterial cultures.

Halloween Cheesy Treats

Makes 4 bite-sized treats

This is a quick and interesting treat you can make for Halloween. Or try one of the variations any time.

1 unwrapped cheese single
1 tablespoon canned pumpkin

1. Place the square of cheese on a microwave-safe plate. Cut it in half.

2. Spread the pumpkin on one half of the cheese, covering the entire piece.

3. Place the other half of the cheese on top of the pumpkin, creating a cheese sandwich with pumpkin in the middle.

4. Cut this cheese sandwich into four equal pieces, spreading them out just a little on the plate.

5. Microwave for 5 to 10 seconds (the time will depend on your microwave) until the cheese softens but does not melt and change shape.

6. Offer one piece of the treat at a time to your cat. If any are left over, store in the refrigerator. Rewarm in the microwave for a few seconds before serving.

Cheesy Treats with Canned Cat Food: Although the smell of warm canned cat food might not appeal to you, I bet your cat will enjoy it! Use a spoonful of your cat's favorite canned cat food in place of the canned pumpkin. Using a fork, poke several holes in the cheese before microwaving so the smells of the warm cat food ooze out, tempting your kitty.

Cheesy Treats with Leftover Meat: Cats love meat! Use some chicken, turkey, beef, or other leftover meat. Just shred or chop the meat into tiny pieces before placing it on the cheese. Using a fork, poke holes in the cheese before microwaving so that the meaty smells come out.

Extra Cheesy Treats: For cats who really go wild for cheese, place a different type of cheese inside the cheese sandwich. For example, use American cheese on the top and bottom with a piece of Swiss cheese or cheddar inside. Try some different cheeses, such as feta or mozzarella, with a shake of dried Parmesan on top.

Thanksgiving Turkey and Rice

Sharing your Thanksgiving dinner with pets is not a good idea; the food is too rich, and gastrointestinal upset is a bad way to end a good day. However, you can make these treats ahead of time and share them with your feline friends on Thanksgiving. One note: When shopping for the baby food, read the labels. Some baby food meats contain spices and seasonings, including onions, which are bad for cats! Make sure you get a baby food that has no such added ingredients.

1 2.5-ounce jar turkey baby food
1 tablespoon sweet potato baby food
1 tablespoon finely grated carrots
1 cup rice flour
1 large egg
1 tablespoon water drained from a can of albacore tuna in water

1. Preheat the oven to 350 degrees.

2. In a mixing bowl, combine all the ingredients, mixing well.

3. Form the dough into balls about ½ teaspoon in size and place them on a greased cookie sheet.

4. Bake 8 to 9 minutes or until the bottoms of the treats are golden brown.

5. Remove from the oven, let cool thoroughly, and store in an airtight container in the refrigerator.

Crunchier Treats: If your cat loves crunchier treats, when all the cookies have been baked, turn off the oven. Place all the cookies back on a cookie sheet and return them to the oven. Leave the cookies in the cooling oven for several hours or overnight.

Nutritional Notes: Carrots

Carrots may have been one of the first foods domesticated by people. Native to Asia, wild carrots were (and still are) small, stringy, and tough to chew. Domesticated carrots are found in a variety of lengths, widths, and sweetnesses. Carrots are great nutritionally, and although cats do not enjoy plain carrots, most cats do like the taste and texture of carrots in foods and treats.

1 medium-sized raw carrot contains:

- 30 calories
- 1 gram protein
- 0 grams fat
- 7 grams carbohydrates
- 25 mg sodium
- 20 mg calcium
- 32 mg phosphorus
- 2,000 RE vitamin A
- 7 mg vitamin C

Thanksgiving Treats

Makes 12 tablespoon-sized treats

You can make these treats with leftover turkey from your meal or from ground turkey.

½ cup cooked turkey
1 tablespoon finely grated carrots
3 tablespoons water drained from a can of albacore tuna in water
3 tablespoons canned pumpkin
3 tablespoons high-quality dry cat food

1. Place all the ingredients in a food processor or blender. Grind for 15 seconds and then puree for an additional 5 seconds.

2. To serve, spoon the desired portion (a teaspoonful for a kitten or a tablespoonful for an adult cat) into your cat's bowl.

3. Store in an airtight container in the refrigerator for up to 1 week. Freeze any excess and thaw before serving.

NUTRITIONAL NOTES: CANNED PUMPKIN

Most cats enjoy the taste of plain canned pumpkin, the kind without added spices. Although this might seem to be a strange thing for cats to eat, for a treat or treat ingredient, it's healthy, nutritious, and a good source of fiber.

½ cup of pureed canned pumpkin contains:

- 42 calories
- 1 gram protein
- less than 1 gram fat
- 25 grams carbohydrates
- 6 mg sodium
- 2 grams fiber

Christmas Cracked Wheat and Catnip

❧ Makes 50 or more bite-sized treats ❧

As a catnip enthusiast, Simon, a 12-year-old blue point mixed-breed cat, rolled in these treats, played pat-pat with them, and when tired of playing, ate them. He purred as he munched on them.

1 14-ounce box Krusteaz Cracked Wheat Bread Mix
¼ cup dried catnip
1 cup warm water
¼ cup dried catnip, for sprinkling on treats

1. Preheat the oven to 400 degrees.

2. Empty bread mix and its yeast packet into a mixing bowl.

3. Add the ¼ cup of catnip to the bread mix and yeast, mixing well.

4. Add the warm water and mix. The dough will be sticky.

5. Drop all the dough onto a greased cookie sheet. Flour or oil your hands so that you can handle the dough and spread it over the bottom of the cookie sheet until it is between ¼ and ½ inch thick.

6. Sprinkle the dough liberally with the remaining ¼ cup catnip.

7. Bake for 10 to 15 minutes or until the bottom of the bread is golden brown. Flip the bread over (don't worry if it breaks) and bake for another 5 to 10 minutes or until both sides are golden brown.

8. Remove from the oven, let cool thoroughly, break into bite-sized pieces, and store in an airtight container in the refrigerator.

TREATS AND TIDBITS: CAT TREATS AS GIFTS

Do some of your friends or family members share their homes with cats? Cat treats make great gifts, especially when given in an appropriately decorated bag, box, or tin.

Before making any treats, find out whether your friend's cat has any food preferences or sensitivities. This is easy enough to do if you plan ahead. Before the holidays, just make up a batch of cat treats—perhaps your cat's favorite recipe—and share them. Then in conversation, talk about cats, cat foods, likes and dislikes, allergies, and so on. You can find out a lot in casual conversation because people like to talk about their cats.

Once you have this information, you can choose a recipe best suited to your friend's cat. Although many recipes can be frozen, most are better fresh, so make up the treats just prior to the time you want to give the gift. The week before is best.

You can package the treats in an airtight container or bag and then place them in a decorated bag, box, or tin. Festive ribbon adds a nice touch, as do some seasonal silk flowers. Use the ribbon to add a catnip mouse, a large feather, or another cat toy.

A gift tag on the tin could name the recipe and list the ingredients. (This is especially important for cats with food sensitivities.) The gift tag should also list the source of the recipe (this book!), and the gift package could even contain a copy of the book!

Christmas Kitty Canes

This is a fun recipe to make, both as treats for your cat and as gifts for feline-owning friends.

½ cup goat's milk
1 tablespoon dried catnip
1½ cups all-purpose flour
¼ teaspoon baking powder
¼ teaspoon salt
⅓ cup powdered chicken bouillon
1 large egg
1 teaspoon red food coloring or a red dye alternative (optional)
¼ cup flour, for rolling out treats

1. Preheat the oven to 350 degrees.

2. Place the goat's milk in a container with a tight-fitting lid and add the catnip. Seal, shake vigorously, and set aside for a few minutes. You want the milk to pick up the catnip scent and flavor.

3. In a mixing bowl, combine the 1½ cups flour, baking powder, salt, and chicken bouillon.

4. Add the egg and the goat's milk mixture to the dry ingredients, mixing well. If the dough is too sticky, add a little more flour. You need to be able to handle the dough.

5. Form the dough into two balls. Set one aside.

6. Sprinkle the ¼ cup flour on a breadboard. Slightly flatten one ball on the floured breadboard and make an indentation in the top. Drop the food coloring into the hole and then knead the dough again to spread the coloring. (Wear gloves if you don't want to risk staining your hands with the food coloring.)

7. When the dough is well kneaded, divide it into walnut-sized balls.

8. Knead the other ball of dough (without adding food coloring), and then divide it into walnut-sized balls.

9. Roll one piece of the plain dough into a long, narrow piece of dough. Do the same with a red piece of dough.

10. Twist together those two pieces of dough to create a candy cane–looking treat. Trim the ends evenly and place the treat on a greased cookie sheet.

11. Repeat steps 9 and 10 until you've used all the dough.

12. Bake for 10 to 12 minutes or until the bottoms of the treats are golden brown.

13. Remove from the oven, let cool thoroughly, and store in an air-tight container in the refrigerator. Break off pieces to serve your cat.

14. To give as gifts, tie a holiday ribbon around each cane or wrap several canes in plastic wrap, fastened with a gift bow.

Special Goodies for Special Occasions 〰 **67**

4

Spectacular Cats
Deserve Tasty Treats

. . . .

MANY PEOPLE WHO DO NOT SHARE THEIR LIVES WITH CATS BELIEVE THAT CATS ARE UNTRAINABLE. UNFORTUNATELY, MANY CAT OWNERS BELIEVE THE SAME THING. AND MAYBE SOME OF THE MYSTERY SURROUNDING CATS COMES FROM THE FACT THAT THEY JUST SEEM TO DO THEIR OWN THING WHILE LIVING WITH US.

CATS CAN BE TRAINED, HOWEVER, AND THAT DOESN'T DIMINISH THEM IN ANY WAY. INSTEAD, TRAINING SHOULD SIMPLY BE ANOTHER FACET OF OUR RELATIONSHIP WITH OUR CATS. CATS ARE FULLY CAPABLE OF LEARNING WHAT BEHAVIOR IS ALLOWED OR NOT ALLOWED, AND THEY CAN ALSO LEARN MANY TRICKS. TRAINING SHOULD BE FUN—FOR YOU AND FOR YOUR CAT—AND SOMETHING BOTH OF YOU LOOK FORWARD TO AND ENJOY.

TRAINING A CAT SHOULD NEVER BE FORCEFUL. INSTEAD, IT SHOULD BE VERY POSITIVE, USING GOOD TREATS AS BOTH LURES AND REWARDS. THE TREATS USED FOR TRAINING SHOULD BE TREATS THE CAT REALLY, REALLY LIKES, SO WHEN YOU FIND A COUPLE RECIPES THAT YOUR CAT IS EXCITED ABOUT, KEEP THOSE TREATS ON HAND FOR TRAINING SESSIONS. THE TREATS SHOULD ALSO BE VERY SMALL; YOU DON'T WANT YOUR CAT TO GET TOO FULL TOO SOON. YOU CAN OFFER THE TREATS ON A SMALL SPOON OR THE END OF A POPSICLE STICK.

IN ADDITION TO THE TREATS LISTED HERE, OTHER GOOD TRAINING TREATS INCLUDE WAKE UP, SLEEPYHEAD! IN CHAPTER 1 AND ON THE PROWL! IN CHAPTER 5.

Xena's Favorite Treats

Makes 60 to 70 ¼-teaspoon-sized treats

Xena is a 4-year-old brown-and-black classic tabby. She is very dignified and very proud. But with these treats, she was willing to try lots of new tricks, including "sit," "lie down," "sit up," and "come." And she had fun doing it!

> 1 6-ounce can albacore tuna in oil or water, drained
> ⅔ cup high-quality dry cat food

1. Place the tuna in a small bowl and use a fork to shred it into fine pieces.

2. Place the cat food in a food processor or blender and grind it to a coarse powder. Measure ⅔ cup after grinding.

3. Combine the ground dry cat food with the tuna, mixing well.

4. Chill in the refrigerator for an hour before using.

5. During training sessions, offer ¼ teaspoon of this treat to your cat on the end of a Popsicle stick or on the tip of a small spoon.

6. Store leftovers in an airtight container in the refrigerator for up to 1 week.

Treats and Tidbits: Using Treats as a Lure and Reward

There are many different approaches to training, and every person who works with animals has a unique technique. However, here is an easy way to teach your cat something new using treats as both a lure and a reward.

Invite your cat up on a piece of furniture where he is at least as high as your waist and where he is comfortable. Have ready some treats you know your cat likes in a small bowl. Use a small spoon or a Popsicle stick to offer some of the treats so your cat knows what you have in the bowl.

Let your cat sniff the spoon, then tell him, "Sweetie, sit," as you move the spoon over his head, toward his shoulders. When his hips move into the sitting position, praise him with, "Yeah! Good!" and give him the treat.

When he will sit nicely, usually after several short training sessions, you can teach him to wave. Ask him to sit, and then praise and reward him. Then hold the spoon with the treat just out of reach. When he reaches a front paw toward the spoon, tell him, "Sweetie, wave! Yeah!" and offer him the treat.

Flaxseed Catnip Treats

Flaxseed meal gives cat treats a nutty flavor that most cats really enjoy. When it's paired with catnip . . . well, these treats are eagerly eaten.

> 1¼ cups whole wheat flour
> ⅓ cup nonfat dry milk
> 1 tablespoon flaxseed meal
> 1 large egg
> 2 tablespoons vegetable oil
> ⅓ cup goat's milk
> ¼ cup dried catnip

1. Preheat the oven to 350 degrees.

2. In a mixing bowl, mix together the first three ingredients.

3. Add the remaining ingredients, mixing well.

4. If the dough is too stiff to mix well with a spoon, flour your hands so you can handle the dough without it sticking and knead it.

5. Using a spoon, scoop up ¼-teaspoon-sized bits of the dough. Form each scoop into a small ball and place on a greased cookie sheet.

6. Bake for 5 to 7 minutes or until the bottoms of the treats are golden brown. Flip the treats and bake for a few more minutes or until the treats are golden brown on both sides.

7. Remove from the oven, let cool thoroughly, and store in an airtight container.

Nutritional Notes: Flaxseed

Flaxseeds are tiny, red-brown seeds that are a rich source of anticarcinogens called *lignans*. Flaxseeds are also rich in omega-3 fatty acids. These nutrients have many health benefits for cats, including contributing to a healthy heart. They are also necessary for smooth, supple skin and a shiny coat. The low calories, fat, and sodium make flaxseeds a healthy ingredient for most cat treats.

1 tablespoon of flaxseeds contains:

- 25 calories
- 1 gram protein
- 3 grams fat
- 1.5 grams carbohydrates
- 5 mg sodium

Tuna Training Treats

Ginger, an orange-and-white 6-year-old long-haired mixed breed, chose these treats over any others that were offered. In addition, with these treats as rewards in one 5-minute training session, she learned to wave her right paw when she heard "Wave!"

1 6-ounce can albacore tuna in oil or water, undrained
½ cup whole wheat flour
½ cup good-quality dry cat food
½ cup nonfat dry milk
1 large egg
¼ cup water
¼ cup catnip, for sprinkling on treats

1. Preheat the oven to 350 degrees.

2. Place the tuna in a mixing bowl. Use a fork to shred the tuna into fine pieces.

3. Add to the tuna all the remaining ingredients except the catnip, mixing well. The dough will be sticky.

4. Using a ¼ teaspoon measuring spoon, scoop bite-sized treats and place on a greased cookie sheet.

5. Sprinkle all the treats with dried catnip.

6. Bake for 10 minutes or until the treats are golden brown.

7. Flip the treats and bake for another 5 minutes or until the treats are golden brown on both sides.

8. When the cookies have been baked, turn off the oven. Put all the cookies back on a cookie sheet and return them to the oven. Leave them in the cooling oven for several hours or overnight to harden.

9. Store leftovers in an airtight container in the refrigerator for up to 1 week.

The Ultimate Training Treats

Not only did all my cats like these treats, but during training sessions with my kitties, my three dogs sat close by, minding their manners, drooling, and hoping to share the fun!

½ cup raw hamburger
¼ cup finely grated cheddar cheese
¼ cup dried catnip

1. In a mixing bowl, combine all the ingredients, mixing well.

2. Form pea-sized treats and place on a cookie sheet that will fit into your freezer.

3. Place the cookie sheet in the freezer until the treats are frozen, usually a couple hours.

4. Remove the treats from the cookie sheet and store them in an airtight container in the freezer.

5. Keep treats frozen until just before use.

TREATS AND TIDBITS: FEEDING UNCOOKED MEATS TO YOUR CAT

Feeding your cat uncooked meats carries some risk, although cats did originally (and still do) hunt and then eat their prey. To minimize the risks, make sure you buy good-quality meat from a reputable supplier. Keep the meat refrigerated until preparation, prepare it quickly, and then return it to the refrigerator or freezer. Training sessions for cats should be very short, so keeping the meat out of the freezer for a few minutes is fine. Be sure to return any leftovers to the freezer.

Sardine Spectacular

Makes 30 to 40 training-sized treats

Sardines are not always the most appealing food to humans, although many people do enjoy them. Many cats love them, however, so they can be a great training motivator.

1 3.75-ounce can sardines in oil, undrained
½ cup plain, unseasoned bread crumbs

1. Place the sardines and their oil in a food processor or blender and puree to a thick paste. (Add a tablespoon or two of water if the fish doesn't form a paste.)

2. Place the paste in a mixing bowl and add the bread crumbs. Stir well to mix thoroughly.

3. Place the mixture in an airtight container in the refrigerator for at least 1 hour.

4. During training, serve tiny bits on the end of a small spoon or a Popsicle stick.

5. Store in an airtight container in the refrigerator for up to 1 week. Extra treats can be formed into bite-sized treats and frozen.

TREATS AND TIDBITS: THE FELINE SENSE OF SMELL

Very few studies have been conducted on the feline sense of smell; many more have been done on dogs. However, experts and cat owners alike know that cats do have a very good sense of smell. Their sense of smell is so good that most cats will not eat a food that doesn't smell right. In addition, a cat with an upper respiratory problem that includes a runny nose may not eat because he either cannot smell his food or the illness has affected his sense of smell.

Therefore, training treats must smell really, really good to be effective. A treat that tastes good but doesn't have an appealing smell will be significantly less motivating than one that smells appealing.

Chicken on the Prowl

This recipe uses Prowl, a dehydrated cat food made by The Honest Kitchen (see page 23).

⅓ cup Prowl
⅓ cup warm water
1 cup cooked chicken

1. Place the Prowl in a small bowl. Add the warm water, stir, and allow the Prowl to rehydrate for 5 minutes.

2. Use a fork to shred the cooked chicken into small pieces.

3. Add the chicken to the rehydrated Prowl and stir well.

4. Refrigerate for at least 1 hour.

5. During training, serve as training treats on a small spoon or the tip of a Popsicle stick.

6. Store leftovers in an airtight container in the refrigerator for up to 1 week. Extra treats can be formed into bite-sized treats and frozen.

Treats and Tidbits: Setting Realistic Training Goals

· ·

We have all seen cats on television commercials doing some amazing things. When we look at our own cats, though, we tend to think they are somehow less capable. They're not! Cats are very intelligent beings and capable of learning a variety of behaviors. For example, my cats can open all the kitchen cupboards as well as the bathroom and linen closet doors. I didn't teach them; they taught themselves and each other.

When deciding what to teach your cat, begin with something easy so that you can gain some training experience yourself and so that you and your cat can both succeed. Then play with your training. Decide what would be fun and then go for it! Just keep in mind that those cats on the television commercial had lots of help—like camera angles, more than one take, and even stand-in cats!

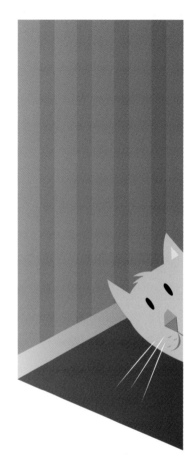

5

Scrumptious Snacks for Special-Needs Kitties

It's not unusual for some cats to have food-related likes and dislikes. Some cats like certain foods more than others. My oldest cat, Squirt, loves anything with tuna in it, and my middle cat, Havoc, will only eat crunchy foods.

Some cats have special dietary requirements due to health issues, including allergies and intolerances. Some health problems, such as kidney or liver disease, require some dietary restrictions, so make sure to talk with your veterinarian about any specific guidelines for your cat.

This chapter has a variety of recipes for felines who must avoid certain ingredients, including wheat-free treats and milk-free snacks. There are also recipes for cats who need some extra nutrition; ailing or recuperating cats are often reluctant to eat. In addition, I've included a couple recipes to tempt kittens to eat.

As with all the other recipes in this book, remember that these are not recipes for daily diets but are treats and should not make up more than 10% of your cat's daily dietary intake.

Treats to Tempt the Finicky Eater

Finicky eaters are usually healthy cats who are unenthusiastic about their food. Some just have tiny appetites, while others use this power over their pet parents to get what they want. Other finicky cats have strong likes and dislikes about specific foods or ingredients.

Some other tempting recipes include Simply Special Sardines and Chicken Liver Pate in chapter 1, Frozen Tuna Cow in chapter 3, The Ultimate Training Treats and Chicken on the Prowl in chapter 4, and Savory Salmon later in this chapter.

Finicky Feline's Chicken

This treat is made of good foods and is excellent for tempting a finicky eater.

¼ cup finely chopped broccoli flowers
¼ cup finely grated carrots
1 cup shredded cooked chicken
½ cup chicken broth

1. Place the broccoli and carrots on a wet paper towel on a microwave-safe dish. Microwave for 10 to 15 seconds—just long enough to warm and slightly steam the vegetables.

2. In a small bowl, mix the shredded chicken and vegetables. Add enough chicken broth to moisten the mixture.

3. Serve a warm ¼-cup serving in your cat's bowl.

4. Store leftovers in an airtight container in the refrigerator. Warm before serving.

Finicky Feline's Chicken and Rice: Some cats don't like the strong smell and taste of broccoli, so for those cats, you can substitute ¼ cup cooked rice for the broccoli.

Finicky Feline's Chicken and Green Beans: If your cat doesn't like broccoli but needs fiber, substitute ¼ cup finely chopped, steamed green beans for the broccoli.

Finicky Feline's Beef: If your cat seems tired of chicken, substitute shredded cooked beef and beef broth for the chicken and chicken broth.

Something Out of the Ordinary: A finicky eater may need something out of the ordinary to tempt the appetite. In such a case, try substituting duck, goose, or venison for the chicken.

Crescent Nibbles

ꞏ Makes about 200 ½-inch treats ꞏ

These treats are quick and easy to make, and your cat will love them.

> 2 cups high-quality dry cat food
> 1 can crescent rolls

1. Preheat the oven to 350 degrees.

2. Place the dry cat food in a food processor or blender and grind to a coarse powder. Measure 2 cups after grinding. Spread on a breadboard.

3. Open the can of crescent rolls and separate the dough into eight individual triangles.

4. One at a time, place each triangle flat on the breadboard, pressing it into the dry cat food so that the cat food sticks to the dough. Turn over the dough and repeat so that the cat food coats both sides of the dough.

5. Place the coated triangles on a greased cookie sheet.

6. Bake for 5 minutes.

7. Flip the treats and bake for 5 more minutes.

8. Remove from the oven, let cool thoroughly, cut into ½-inch pieces, and store in an airtight container.

Nibbles with Different Cat Foods: Although you can make this recipe with the dry cat food your cat eats regularly, it will be more appealing if you vary the dry cat food used. Many stores offer samples of different cat foods; use one of those sample bags when you make this recipe.

Parmesan Cheese Nibbles: Decrease the dry cat food by ½ cup and add ½ cup canned grated Parmesan cheese to the dry cat food on the breadboard.

Catnip Nibbles: Decrease the dry cat food by ½ cup and add ½ cup dried catnip to the dry cat food on the breadboard.

TREATS AND TIDBITS: TAURINE

Listen to a few cat food commercials, and you'll hear, "This food is an excellent source of taurine!" So what is taurine, and why is it so important for your cat?

Taurine is an amino acid that is found in milk, brewer's yeast, eggs, fish, and red meat. A diet deficient in taurine can lead to vision problems and heart disease. Unfortunately, for many years dry cat foods lacked taurine, leading to many cats experiencing serious health problems. Since the mid-1970s, however, cat food manufacturers have been adding taurine to their foods.

Coaxing the Reluctant Eater

Although some kittens are excellent eaters, others are not, especially orphans and those weaned too early. Invalids and cats who don't feel well can also be horrible eaters. Long-time cat breeders, veterinarians, and those wonderful people involved in cat rescue have used their own favorite glop recipes for years. (It's called *glop* because it makes the noise "glop" when dropped into a bowl!) Here are three recipes I have used successfully with numerous rescued kittens and feline invalids.

Savory Salmon

Tinkerbell, a 6-year-old long-haired Persian mix, is a known finicky eater. During our taste tests, she turned up her little nose at many treats, but she eagerly ate these.

   1 7-ounce can salmon in oil, undrained
   1 cup cooked brown rice
   ⅓ cup finely chopped cat grass (usually oat grass)

1. Place the salmon and its oil in a mixing bowl and use a fork to shred it into small pieces.

2. Add the remaining ingredients and mix well.

3. To serve, spoon the desired portion (a teaspoonful for a kitten or a tablespoonful for an adult cat) into your cat's bowl.

4. Store leftovers in an airtight container in the refrigerator for up to 1 week.

Savory Salmon with Veggies: If you don't have any cat grass, you can substitute the same amount of finely diced broccoli flowers or pureed green beans for the grass.

Goat's Milk Glop

∽☙ Makes 8 ¼-cup servings ❧∾

Goat's milk is more easily digested by most cats than cow's milk, and it rarely causes gastrointestinal upset.

1 cup water
1 envelope unflavored gelatin
1 cup goat's milk
1 tablespoon water drained from a can of albacore tuna in water

1. Place the water in a microwave-safe bowl and add the gelatin.

2. Place the bowl in the microwave and cook until the water is bubbling well—usually 1 to 2 minutes, depending on your microwave.

3. Remove from microwave and add the remaining ingredients, mixing well.

4. Refrigerate until the gelatin sets, usually a couple hours.

5. To serve, spoon the desired portion (a tablespoon for a young kitten or a ¼ cup for an adult cat) into your cat's bowl.

6. Store leftovers in an airtight container in the refrigerator for up to 1 week.

Baby Food Glop: Not all cats are tuna aficionados, so if your cat likes other meats, you can use baby food. Instead of the tuna water, use a 2.5-ounce jar of meat baby food, such as turkey or chicken.

Canned Cat Food Glop: Are there a couple types of canned cat food that really tempt your cat? Instead of the tuna water, use a tablespoon of a high-quality canned cat food.

Clam Juice Glop: Do you have a recipe or two you enjoy that use canned clams? When you make one of those for yourself, save the clam juice and make your cat a very special treat. Substitute 1 tablespoon of the water from a can of clams for the tuna water.

NUTRITIONAL NOTES: GOAT'S MILK

Many cats are lactose intolerant, especially as adults, which means they are unable to properly digest cow's milk. If these cats drink cow's milk, gastrointestinal upset (gas, bloating, diarrhea, and even vomiting) may result. However, most cats can digest goat's milk quite well, with no unpleasant side effects. Most cats also like the taste of goat's milk.

1 cup of goat's milk contains:

- 168 calories
- 9 grams protein
- 7 grams fat
- 11 grams carbohydrates
- 120 mg sodium
- 327 mg calcium
- 271 mg phosphorus
- 498 mg potassium

Pedialyte Glop

Makes 8 to 9 ¼-cup servings

Pedialyte (a pediatric electrolyte formula) is designed to use when a human baby is not eating or drinking, has diarrhea, or is vomiting. Kittens and ailing cats who are not eating well or old cats who don't feel well can also use the benefits of this formula.

1 3-ounce can albacore tuna in oil or water, drained
1 cup unflavored Pedialyte
1 envelope unflavored gelatin
1 cup goat's milk
⅓ cup plain, unflavored yogurt with live, active cultures
1 tablespoon molasses

1. Use a fork to shred the tuna well; set the tuna aside.

2. Place the Pedialyte in a microwave-safe bowl and add the gelatin.

3. Place the bowl in the microwave and cook until the mixture is bubbling well—usually 1 to 2 minutes, depending on your microwave.

4. Remove from the microwave and add the remaining ingredients, including the shredded tuna, mixing well.

5. Refrigerate until the gelatin sets, usually a couple hours.

6. To serve, spoon the desired portion (a tablespoon for a young kitten or a ¼ cup for an adult cat) into your cat's bowl.

7. Store leftovers in an airtight container in the refrigerator for up to 1 week.

Nutritional Notes: Pediatric Electrolyte Formula

A pediatric electrolyte formula, one of which is marketed as Pedialyte, is a water-based formula designed to prevent dehydration and to restore the body's water balance, electrolytes, and minerals. Pediatric formulas can be found in the infant or first-aid sections of grocery stores and drug stores.

A liter of pediatric electrolyte formula in a water base contains the following:

- 100 calories
- 45 mg sodium
- 20 mg potassium
- 35 mg chloride
- 30 mg citrate
- 25 grams dextrose

Wheat-Free Treats

Cats are carnivores, designed to eat meat. Although grains are common ingredients in almost all dry, kibble-type cat foods, some cats have trouble digesting certain grains. Others develop allergies to some grains, especially wheat. If a cat has been diagnosed with a wheat allergy, wheat should not be present in any of the cat's foods or treats.

Several wheat-free recipes can be found in this book: In chapter 1: Quick and Easy Treats, Simply Special Sardines, Chicken Liver Pate, and Bountiful Banana Treats; in chapter 2: Salmon Soy Circles; in chapter 3: Frozen Tuna Cow, Thanksgiving Turkey and Rice, Happy Birthday Catnip Tea, and Squirt's Favorite Birthday Treat; in chapter 4: The Ultimate Training Treats, Sardine Spectacular, and Chicken on the Prowl; and earlier in this chapter: Savory Salmon.

Here are some additional treats that contain no wheat.

Turkey and Parmesan Crumbles

Cedar, a 4-year-old, pastel brown tabby, ate this treat with passion! He took one sniff, and the treat disappeared.

1 cup crumbled cooked ground turkey
¼ cup canned grated Parmesan cheese
¼ teaspoon brewer's yeast
⅓ cup flaxseed meal
⅓ cup oat flour

1. Preheat the oven to 350 degrees.

2. Place the crumbled cooked turkey in a food processor or blender and puree until smooth. If needed, add just enough water to process the meat.

3. Place the pureed meat in a bowl and add the remaining ingredients. The dough will be dry and crumbly.

4. Spread the crumbles evenly on a greased cookie sheet.

5. Bake for 5 to 7 minutes or until dry.

6. Serve by the teaspoon as treats or sprinkle a little over a teaspoon of yogurt or cottage cheese.

7. Store leftovers in an airtight container in the refrigerator for up to 2 weeks.

Lamb and Rice Bites

⌒ Makes about 50 ½-teaspoon-sized treats ⌒

Havoc, an 11-year-old Russian Blue, doesn't like canned cat foods or any soft foods; he likes crunchy treats. This recipe is one of his favorites.

1 2.5-ounce jar lamb baby food
½ cup rice flour
1 tablespoon finely grated carrots
1 large egg

1. Preheat the oven to 350 degrees.

2. In a mixing bowl, combine all the ingredients, mixing well. The dough will be sticky.

3. Drop by ½ teaspoon onto a greased cookie sheet.

4. With a floured knife, score each treat once or twice, so the treat can be broken into two or four pieces after it is baked.

5. Bake about 5 minutes or until the bottoms of the treats are golden brown.

6. Flip the treats and bake for another 3 minutes or until both sides of the treats are golden brown.

7. Remove from the oven, let cool thoroughly, break along scored lines to make bite-sized treats, and store in an airtight container in the refrigerator.

Crunchier Treats: If your cat loves crunchier treats, when all the cookies have been baked, turn off the oven. Place all the cookies back on a cookie sheet and return them to the oven. Leave the cookies in the cooling oven for several hours or overnight.

NUTRITIONAL NOTES: EGGS

Nutritionists call eggs the "perfect food." They have been given a biological value of 100%, and all other sources of proteins are measured against eggs. Although some other foods have more protein, eggs, unlike other protein sources, have all the essential amino acids needed for good nutrition.

1 medium chicken egg contains:

- 9 grams protein
- 5.6 grams fat
- 0 grams fiber
- trace carbohydrates
- 72 mg sodium
- 67 mg potassium
- 29 mg calcium
- 103 mg phosphorus

Tuna and Oat Snacks

⌒☁ Makes 40 to 60 bite-sized treats ☁⌒

These treats are not only wheat free, but also lactose free, and consequently they are great for cats on restricted diets.

 1 6-ounce can albacore tuna in water, drained
 1 cup oat flour
 ¼ teaspoon baking powder
 ¼ teaspoon salt
 1 large egg
 ¼ teaspoon old-fashioned oats (not quick or instant oats)

1. Preheat the oven to 350 degrees.

2. In a mixing bowl, combine all the ingredients, mixing thoroughly.

3. Spread the dough on the bottom of a greased cookie sheet in a thin layer.

4. Bake for 7 minutes or until the treats are golden brown.

5. Flip the treats (don't worry about breaking the dough) and bake for another 7 minutes or until the treats are golden brown on both sides.

6. Remove from the oven, let cool thoroughly, break into bite-sized pieces, and store in an airtight container in the refrigerator.

On the Prowl!

These treats are made using Prowl, a dehydrated cat food made by The Honest Kitchen (see page 23). These soft treats are easy to make, very nutritious, and free of cereal grains.

   1 tablespoon Prowl
   2 tablespoons warm water
   1 tablespoon plain yogurt

1. Place the Prowl in a small bowl. Add the warm water, stir, and allow the Prowl to rehydrate for 5 minutes.

2. Add the yogurt to the rehydrated Prowl and stir well.

3. To serve, spoon the desired portion (a teaspoonful for a kitten or a tablespoonful for an adult cat) into your cat's bowl.

4. Store leftovers in an airtight container in the refrigerator for up to 1 week.

Lactose-Free Treats

Many cats, once they reach adulthood, cannot tolerate cow's milk, so very few recipes in this book contain milk. Most of the recipes that do include milk use goat's milk, which is easily digested by most cats, even lactose-intolerant adult cats. The majority of cats who are lactose intolerant can digest yogurt and cheese, even if it's made from cow's milk.

Many recipes elsewhere in this book contain no dairy at all: In chapter 1: Quick and Easy Treats, Simply Special Sardines, Chicken Liver Pate, and Ooh, la, la, Oysters!; in chapter 2: Basic Kitty Cookies, Chicken Liver Crunchies, Tuna Stars, and Salmon Soy Circles; in chapter 3: Happy Birthday Catnip Tea, Thanksgiving Turkey and Rice, and Thanksgiving Treats; in chapter 4: Chicken on the Prowl; and earlier in this chapter: Savory Salmon.

Krusteaz Egg and Catnip Treats

Makes more than 50 bite-sized treats

The Krusteaz bread mix helps create a soft, chewy treat.

1 14-ounce box Krusteaz White Bread Mix
¼ cup dried catnip
1 large egg
¾ cup warm water
1 egg yolk, beaten
¼ cup dried catnip, for sprinkling on treats

1. Preheat the oven to 400 degrees.

2. In a large mixing bowl, combine the bread mix, the yeast from the bread mix box, and ¼ cup catnip.

3. Stir in the egg and water. Mix well to form a sticky dough.

4. Place the dough on a greased cookie sheet. Flour or oil your hands so that you can handle the dough, and then spread the dough over the bottom of the cookie sheet until it is ¼ to ½ inch thick.

5. Using a pastry brush or a spoon, spread the beaten egg yolk over the top of the dough. Sprinkle the dough with the remaining ¼ cup of dried catnip.

6. Bake for 10 to 15 minutes or until the bottom of the treat is golden brown.

7. Flip the treat (don't worry if it breaks apart) and bake for another 5 to 10 minutes or until both sides of the treat are golden brown.

8. Remove from the oven, let cool thoroughly, break into bite-sized pieces, and store in an airtight container.

Vegetable Soup

⌐☜ Makes 2 ¼-cup servings ☞⌐

This is a very different type of treat, and some cats may initially be wary of it. Once they taste it, however, most will lap it up with gusto.

1 extra-large vegetable bouillon cube
½ cup water
1 tablespoon finely grated carrot
1 tablespoon fresh, finely chopped mint (optional)
1 tablespoon fresh, finely chopped catnip

1. Place the vegetable bouillon cube in a bowl and add the water. Microwave for 1 to 2 minutes or until the water is hot and the bouillon cube has dissolved.

2. Place the bowl in the refrigerator to cool.

3. Mix together the carrot, mint (if desired), and catnip.

4. When the bouillon has cooled, add the carrot mixture to the bouillon.

5. Serve a room temperature ¼-cup serving in your cat's bowl.

6. Store leftovers in an airtight container in the refrigerator.

NUTRITIONAL NOTES:
VEGETABLE BOUILLON

• •

Some vegetable bouillons contain salt and seasonings, including onions, garlic, and spices. Avoid these and instead look for bouillons that contain just vegetables, usually carrots, cabbage, parsley, and sometimes corn.

Index

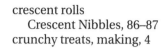

Free! Feline chef accessories!

Your furry friends will really be purring with these free feline chef accessories that make catering to them even more fun! To receive your FREE Feline Chef accessories, simply mail in this form and get:

1. A measuring spoon
2. A recipe card with a great recipe from the book
3. Goodie bags for sharing fabulous treats

Recipe card

Measuring spoon

Gift bags.

Howell Book House®
An Imprint of
Ⓦ**WILEY**

To receive your **FREE** gift:

1) Complete and submit this form or include the information on a 3x5 card.

2) Send the completed form with your cash register receipt(s); photocopy accepted.

3) Wait 6-8 weeks for delivery.

Send to:

Feline Chef Accessory Free Gift
Dept. 43, Offer # OWGR00003
P.O. Box 10003-43
Douglas, AZ 85655-1103